ALISON HOLST'S

MARVELLOUS
MUFFINS

Published by Hyndman Publishing
PO Box 5017, Dunedin
ISBN 0-9583401-0-2
© Text: Alison Holst
Designers: Rob Di Leva, Alison Holst
Production: Di Leva Design
Illustrator: Clare Ferguson
Photography: Sal Criscillo,
page 51 by Sharon Hogg
Home Economists: Alison Holst,
Jane Ritchie, Dee Harris, Keryn Wear
Cover Props: Levene & Co. Ltd.
Printing: Tablet Colour Print
14th Reprint January 1998

The recipes in this book have been carefully tested by the
author. The publisher and the author have made every
effort to ensure that the instructions are accurate and safe,
but they cannot accept liability for any resulting injury or
loss or damage to property whether direct or
consequential.

Because ovens and microwave ovens vary so much, you
should use the cooking times suggested in recipes as guides
only. The first time you make a recipe, check it at intervals
to make sure it is not cooking faster, or more slowly than
expected.

Always follow the detailed instructions given by the
manufacturers of your appliances and equipment, rather
than the more general instructions given in these recipes.

Acknowledgements

We wish to thank the following for
providing their products for recipe
testing and photography:

ALISON'S CHOICE for dried fruits
and nuts, brans, wheat germ, seeds,
icing sugar, choco chips

BARKERS for Horseradish Sauce

BENNICKS POULTRY FARM -
Buller Rd, Levin for fresh eggs

CHARLES PETERSON (ACTON
INTERNATIONAL) for Ocean
Spray Cranberry Sauce

COUNTRY FOODS (N.Z.) LTD
for Country Goodness Sour Cream
and Cream Cheese, Anchor Grated
Tasty Cheddar, Swiss Maid Yoghurt

EMPIRE FOODSTUFFS for dried
herbs and spices

FERNDALE DAIRIES for Parmesan
Cheese and Galaxy Blue Vein Cheese

KIWI BACON COMPANY for
bacon and ham

J. WATTIE FOODS for canned
vegetables and fruit

LEVENE & CO. LTD for tablewear
for cover photograph

SEASMOKE for smoked salmon

S.C. JOHNSON & SON PTY
LIMITED for Chef Mate®

WILLIAM AITKEN & CO. Azalea
Grapeseed Oil and Lupi Olive Oil

For current prices and information
about Alison's Swiss Knives, send a
self addressed envelope to:

ALISON HOLST'S MAIL ORDERS
PO BOX 17016
WELLINGTON

Chef Mate® is a registered trademark of S.C. Johnson & Son Inc U.S.A.
Authorised User: S.C. Johnson & Son Pty Ltd, Mahunga Drive, Mangere, Auckland, New Zealand.

Contents

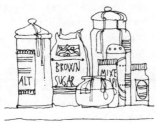

Measures for Muffins

For best results use standard metric cups and spoons for these recipes. Wherever possible the ingredients have been measured rather than weighed, and the quantities given in level cup and spoon measures.

A standard metric measuring cup holds 250 millilitres (quarter of a litre). Clear plastic measuring cups with a pouring lip and with the one cup mark below the rim are the best cups to use for measuring liquids. They should be marked with quarter cup divisions, and also with 50-millilitre divisions.

Buy a set of single capacity measuring cups to measure dry ingredients quickly and easily.

When you measure flour, fill the single capacity cups lightly, and level it off, without shaking or banging the measure, since this packs down the flour and means that too much is used in the recipe.

Most butter quantities have been given by weight. Butter packs have 50g or 100g markings on them. These are accurate, apart from the markings at each end of the pack. Small quantities of butter have been measured by spoons - one tablespoon of butter weighs 15 g.

Use a set of metric measuring spoons when cooking with metricated recipes.

One tablespoon holds 15 millilitres, and one teaspoon holds five millilitres.

All the cup and spoon measures in this book are level, unless otherwise stated. Golden syrup, honey and treacle are the exceptions. For convenience use rounded household spoonfuls of these. Dip spoon in boiling water first. Remember that a heaped teaspoon can hold twice as much as a level one, and will upset the balance of the ingredients used in a recipe. The following abbreviations have been used in this book:

cm	centimetre
C	Celsius
ml	millilitre
g	gram
tsp	teaspoon
Tbsp	tablespoon

Why make muffins ?

Muffins are SO versatile! They are a treat for a late weekend breakfast and the perfect accompaniment for morning or afternoon tea or coffee. Savoury muffins can be the main part of a lunch or light weekend evening meal, and richer or fresh fruit muffins make wonderful desserts. Mini-muffins are quite at home at cocktail parties, and muffins of all flavours and sizes are a welcome addition to packed lunches and picnic meals.

But, that's not all! Muffins make great gifts! A basket of muffins will thank a teacher, greet a new neighbour, welcome home the mother of a new baby, cheer an ill or elderly acquaintance, help raise funds for your church, kindy or school, ...and will probably make you new friends, into the bargain.

Once you have mastered the finer points of muffin making, your muffins are likely to make your reputation as a baker. They might also provide you with pocket money or start you off on a flourishing career. What about taking a big basket containing a selection of warm, freshly baked muffins to a nearby business. Arrive at morning teatime, or at the start of a lunch break, especially on Monday! If your muffins are tempting enough, your customers are likely to want more muffins to take home at the end of their working day. You may find you have a tiger by the tail! Is it easy to make really good muffins? Yes! Are they expensive to make? No. Basic muffins, and many varieties are not, and most of the muffins which sound luxurious and expensive contain only small amounts of "gourmet" ingredients.

Muffins are very fast and easy to mix and make, requiring the minimum of equipment. Muffins vary in size, shape, and flavour. They need never become boring, because it is so easy to "ring the changes". Basic muffins require very few ingredients, and you are sure to have these in your pantry and refrigerator.

It takes only a little practice to become a muffin expert - to get the "feel" of muffin mixtures, and to make really marvellous muffins every time you make a batch. Even if you have tried the occasional sweet muffin, you may never have thought about making savoury muffins for the main part of a light meal, or to accompany soup or a salad. I hope this book will encourage you to try many types of muffin, then to invent new ones of your own. Good muffin cooking!

June, 1994

Mini, Medium or Monster Muffins?

You can buy muffin pans of varying sizes. Whatever you buy, make sure it has a good non-stick finish, since many muffin mixtures stick badly!

MEDIUM-SIZED MUFFINS

Most widely used are muffin trays which make twelve medium-sized muffins. (The twelve depressions, if filled with water, hold 4 cupfuls altogether.) Most of the recipes in this book will make 12 muffins this size. I put a quarter-cup measure full of mixture into each muffin hole.

You can also buy muffin trays with six holes the size of those above. These fit in most bench-top ovens, and are also handy if you have a little mixture left over, and want to make a few more muffins.

MINI-MUFFINS

Mini-muffin tins are fun! Hardly any one will refuse one of these little muffins which are less than half the size of those above. (A muffin tray holding 12 mini-muffins, if filled with water, holds $1\frac{1}{2}$ cupfuls.) A mixture making 12 medium muffins will make about 30 mini-muffins. Mini-muffins usually need a slightly shorter cooking time - take about two minutes off the time needed for medium muffins. Mini-muffin trays usually fit in bench-top ovens.

MONSTER MUFFINS

Monster-muffins (Texan Muffins) come in trays of six. Each muffin is twice the size of a medium muffin. Muffins from these trays always look extra-generous. (The tray of six holds 5 cups of water altogether.) These muffins usually take 2-4 minutes longer to cook than medium muffins.

SMALL CAKE PANS

If you have no muffin pans, but have pans in which you make small cakes, try them, but don't expect such good results. Muffins from these pans will be flatter and crustier than those made in muffin pans. The pans may need very careful preparation, unless they have a good non-stick finish.

GEM IRONS

If you have gem irons tucked away in a bottom cupboard, by all means try cooking your muffins in them. Heat the irons in the oven as it warms up. Put the hot irons on a heat-resistant surface, brush quickly with melted butter, or spray well with Chef Mate non-stick spray, then drop in the mixture from the side of a dessert spoon. The cooking time will be shorter than for medium muffins.

PAPER CASES

Paper cases the size of medium muffin pans are sometimes used for muffins which are to be sold or handled a lot. Some muffin mixtures stick to the paper badly, and the muffins break as they are removed. Paper cases are helpful for microwaved muffins which otherwise stick to their plastic pans.

To make marvellous muffins

Please take a few minutes to read this page before you make the recipes in this book, even if you are already a muffin maker!

Muffins are very quick and easy - but to make your reputation as a MARVELLOUS muffin maker, you need to know all the finer points!

First, combine the dry ingredients in a bowl big enough to mix all the ingredients later. Sieve them into the bowl, or toss them with a dry whisk or fork once they are in the bowl. However you do it, mix them well, so they are light and airy. Next, mix the liquids in the easiest way. If you need melted butter, warm it in a microwave oven or a pot on the stove, then add the other liquids and the egg and mix with a fork, beater or whisk. Try to finish up with a room-temperature mixture. Extra ingredients, sometimes food processed, may be mixed with the liquids. They are sometimes stirred through the dry mixture, or they may be added separately. Follow the recipe instructions.

The way you combine the dry and wet mixtures is vital. Add all the liquid and extra ingredients at once. *Fold them together with as little mixing as possible.* I use a flexible straight-bladed stirrer/spreader, or a rubber scraper. Slowly bring your stirrer, scraper, fork or spoon down the side of the bowl and under the mixture, then up through it, turning bowl and repeating this until no pockets of flour are left. Stop while the mixture looks rough and lumpy. NEVER give it a quick beat or stir for good measure! Muffins can stick like crazy! Use pans with a non-stick finish, clean these well, but without scratching them, and always use a light, even coating of Chef Mate non-stick spray as an extra precaution.

Spoon muffins into prepared pans, helping the mixture off with another spoon, rather than letting it drop off by itself. Try to divide the mixture evenly - put as few spoonfuls in each pan as possible. Let the mixture mound naturally-do not smooth or interfere with its surface. (Add toppings if you like.)

Bake muffins at a high temperature until the centres spring back when pressed. If this is hard to judge, push a skewer into the centre. When it comes out clean, the muffins are ready. Cooking times are only a guide. The muffins in this book were cooked in an oven with a fan. Without a fan, use higher temperatures or allow more time.

After cooking, let cooked muffins stand in their pans for 3–4 minutes. They loosen themselves in this time! Press down gently on the edges of a muffin with several fingers of one hand, and twist slightly. As soon as the muffin will turn freely, lift it out, and let it finish cooling on a rack.

Muffins are best served warm, soon after baking. They will stay warm for some time, without going soggy, in a napkin-lined basket. Reheat when necessary (take care not to overheat) in a microwave oven, or in a paper bag at about 150°C in a conventional oven.

Champion Cheese Muffins

Everybody loves these muffins and they are easy enough to make often. If you make these muffins regularly buy pre-grated tasty cheese to use in them. This will save you precious minutes as well as the skin on your knuckles.

2 cups (200 g) grated tasty cheese
1½ cups self-raising flour
½ tsp salt
1 Tbsp sugar
pinch of cayenne pepper

1 egg
1 cup milk

Measure the grated cheese, self-raising flour, salt, sugar and cayenne pepper into a large bowl. Mix lightly with your fingertips to combine.

In a small container beat the egg and milk until evenly combined. Pour all the liquid onto the dry ingredients, then fold the two mixtures together, taking care not to over-mix.

Spoon mixture into 12 medium muffin pans, which have been sprayed with Chef Mate non-stick spray.

Optional topping: Sprinkle with a little extra cheese and paprika or chili powder.

Bake at 210°C for about 12 minutes, until muffins spring back when pressed in the middle and are golden brown.

(Read mixing/baking details on page 7)

❦ SIZE: Mini, Medium and Monster ❦ SERVE: Mini for cocktail snacks and ladies afternoon tea, Medium for general use or if making to freeze. Monster muffins make good lunches.

Herbed Mini Muffins

These very special little green-flecked muffins disappear fast at any time of the day. For a special treat or to serve with drinks, split warm herbed mini-muffins, spread them with a little horseradish cream cheese spread, and add a folded slice of smoked salmon.

1 cup flour
2 tsp baking powder
1 cup (100 g) grated tasty cheese
½ cup chopped parsley
1 Tbsp chopped fresh herbs
1 spring onion, chopped
½ tsp salt
1 tsp sugar
⅛ tsp cayenne pepper

1 egg
½ cup + 2 Tbsp milk

Measure together into a large bowl the first 9 ingredients. Use whatever fresh herbs you like best, or whichever will go well with fillings or toppings. (Use dill for salmon, basil for smoked meat.) Toss well to mix.

In another bowl, beat the egg and milk together with a fork or whisk.

Tip the egg mixture into the dry ingredients and fold together, stirring just enough to dampen the flour, etc.

Spoon mixture into 18–24 mini-muffin tins which have been evenly coated with Chef Mate non-stick spray.

Bake at 200°C for 10–12 minutes, until the centres spring back when pressed.

(Read mixing/baking details on page 7)

❦ **SIZE:** Mini, Medium and Monster ❦ **SERVE:** Minis hot, whole, at any time. Split minis and fill with savoury spreads and smoked salmon, thin slices smoked meat etc. as cocktail savouries. Freeze for later use.

Asparagus Luncheon Muffins

Both canned and fresh asparagus give muffins a distinctive flavour. These are unusual and interesting, as well as popular.

2 cups self-raising flour
1 cup (100 g) grated tasty cheese
2 spring onions, chopped
¼ tsp cayenne pepper
½ tsp salt

340 gram can asparagus
¼ cup sour cream
2 eggs

Measure the flour, cheese, spring onions, cayenne pepper and salt into a fairly large bowl. Toss together with a fork to combine.

Drain the asparagus (retain the liquid) and chop stalks into 5mm pieces.

Make the asparagus liquid up to ¾ cup with water if necessary, mix this with the sour cream and eggs in another bowl.

Tip this and the chopped asparagus into the bowl with the dry ingredients. Without overmixing, fold everything together, taking care not to mash the asparagus pieces.

Spray 12 medium sized muffin pans with Chef Mate non-stick spray. Put about ¼ cup of mixture into each muffin cup.

Bake at 200°C for 12–15 minutes, until muffins spring back when pressed.

(Read mixing/baking details on page 7)

VARIATION:
Cut 200 grams of fresh asparagus into 5mm slices, cook until just tender, in about ½ cup of lightly salted water. Use cooking liquid as above.

❦ SIZE: Mini or Medium ❦ SERVE: Warm as fingerfood for parties, as the main part of lunch.

Herbed Pumpkin Muffins

Mashed pumpkin gives these muffins a wonderful colour. An interesting combination of herbs intensifies both the pumpkin and cheese flavours.

2 cups self-raising flour
½ tsp salt
1 Tbsp sugar
2 cups (200 g) grated cheese
1½ tsp cumin
1 tsp oreganum
¼ –½ tsp cayenne pepper

1 egg
1 cup milk
1 cup mashed cooked
*   pumpkin (250 g)*

Measure the first 7 ingredients into a large bowl, crumbling the oreganum a little as you add it. Add cayenne to suit your taste. Toss well, to mix all the dry ingredients thoroughly.

In another container, combine the egg, milk and mashed pumpkin. Beat together to mix well.

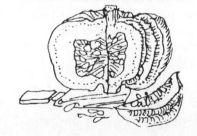

Pour the liquid ingredients into the bowl containing the dry mixture. Without overmixing, fold everything together. The flour should be just dampened, not smooth.

Spray 12 medium sized muffin pans with Chef Mate non-stick spray. Put about ¼ cup of mixture into each muffin cup.

Bake at 220°C for 12–14 minutes, until golden brown and muffins spring back when pressed.

(Read mixing/baking details on page 7).

❧ SIZE: Mini or Medium ❧ TOPPING: Grated cheese, paprika or chili powder, toasted sesame seeds, or pumpkin seeds.
❧ SERVE: Warm as fingerfood for a party, with soup for lunch. See photograph on cover

Bugs Bunny's Best Muffins

You may well find that these vegetable-filled muffins are popular with children who would turn up their noses at single servings of the vegetables in them! The muffins are moist and eggy, easy for toddlers and preschoolers to eat as fingerfood.

1 cup self-raising flour
1½ cups (150 g) grated tasty cheese
2 rashers bacon, cooked and chopped
1 medium onion, finely chopped
¼ cup parsley, finely chopped

4 eggs
½ cup milk
1 cup mashed potato
1 cup mashed pumpkin
½ cup creamed sweetcorn
½ tsp salt

In a large bowl combine the self-raising flour with the grated cheese, chopped bacon (without rinds) finely chopped onion and parsley. Toss together to combine. (Cook the bacon in a pan or in a microwave oven until it loses its rawness. It need not brown.)

In another bowl, beat the egg and milk, then add the (leftover) mashed potato and pumpkin, the sweetcorn and salt. (Add about ½ cup of other finely chopped, well-drained cooked vegetables if you like.)

Combine the two mixtures taking care not to over-mix. Spoon the mixture into about 18 medium-sized muffin pans which have been coated with Chef Mate non-stick spray.

Bake at 180°C for 20–25 minutes or until muffins feel firm when pressed in the centre and are evenly browned. Leave muffins to firm up before carefully removing them from their pans.

Reheat leftovers the next day.

(Read mixing/baking details on page 7).

❦ SIZE: Medium and mini. ❦ SERVE: Warm or hot to replace vegetables at barbecues and family dinners. Serve in packed or "home" lunches. Good fingerfood for small children.

Tutti-Fruity Muffins

Avocado and Bacon Muffins

Avocado & Bacon Muffins

These are some of my most popular muffins. Everybody likes the idea of the combination of avocado, cheese, bacon and spring onions. Serve them with fruit and a drink as a complete lunch.

2 cups flour
4 tsp baking powder
½ tsp salt
1 Tbsp sugar
pinch cayenne pepper
1 cup (100 g) grated tasty cheese
4 spring onions, chopped
3 rashers bacon

75 grams butter
1 egg
1 cup milk
1 avocado
about 1 Tbsp lemon juice

Sieve the first four (dry) ingredients into a large bowl. Add the cayenne pepper, grated cheese and chopped spring onion, and stir to combine.

Chop the bacon finely and cook in a frypan or under the grill until crisp. Keep the bacon drippings.

Melt the butter, add the egg, milk and bacon drippings and beat to combine. Halve the avocado, scoop out the flesh with a dessert or tablespoon, then cut the flesh into 7mm cubes. Sprinkle with lemon juice to stop them from browning. Add to the liquid mixture.

Add the bacon to the liquid ingredients and fold both mixtures together. Stir only to dampen the flour.

Spray 12 medium muffin pans with Chef Mate non-stick spray. Put about ¼ cup in each muffin cup.

Bake at 200°C for about 10 minutes, or until the muffins spring back when pressed lightly in the centre.

(Read mixing/baking details on page 7).

❧ SIZE: Mini and Medium ❧ SERVE: Always warm, as fingerfood with drinks, as the main part of lunch.

Cheesy Red Pepper Muffins

When you roast red peppers, then chop them into a cheesy muffin, you get muffins with
a lovely flavour as well as an attractive red fleck through them.

1½ cups self-raising flour
2 cups (200 g) grated tasty cheese
½ tsp salt
1 Tbsp sugar
pinch cayenne pepper
1–2 Tbsp chopped fresh coriander
    leaf (optional)
1 large red pepper, roasted and
    chopped

1 egg
1 cup milk

Measure into a large bowl the flour, cheese, salt, sugar and cayenne pepper. Add coriander leaf and chopped roasted pepper. Mix lightly with your fingertips to combine.

In another container, beat the egg and milk together, then pour onto the dry ingredients.

Fold together, taking care not to overmix.

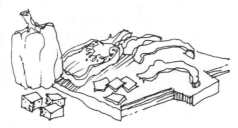

Spoon the mixture, without extra mixing, into non-stick muffin pans that have been sprayed with Chef Mate non-stick spray. Sprinkle with paprika if desired.

Bake at 200°C for about 12 minutes, or until muffins are golden brown and spring back when pressed lightly in the centre.

Remove from oven, stand for 2–3 minutes, then twist muffins carefully to loosen them before removing from the pan.

(Read baking/mixing details on page 7).

🍎 SIZE: Mini or Medium. 🍎 SERVE: Warm, for brunch or lunch or as finger food.

Ham & Celery Muffins

Chop ham and raw celery into muffins to serve with soup for a winter lunch or stuffed eggs and salad in summer. This mixture makes good muffins of any size, but it makes particularly nice mini-muffins.

1¼ cups self-raising flour
1 cup (100 g) grated tasty cheese
½ cup (75 g) cubed ham
½ cup finely chopped celery
2 spring onions, chopped
2 Tbsp chopped parsley

1 egg
¾ cup milk
1 Tbsp grainy mustard

Measure the flour into a large bowl. Prepare the next 5 ingredients, adding each to the bowl with the flour as it is prepared. Buy ham pieces from a supermarket deli, and chop the pieces into 5mm cubes, and the celery into pieces smaller than the ham. Slice the white and green parts of the spring onions finely.

In another bowl beat together the egg, milk and mustard.

Tip the egg mixture into the large bowl, then fold everything together, taking care not to overmix.

Spoon the mixture into 18–24 mini-muffin pans which have been coated with Chef Mate non-stick spray.

Bake at 200°C for 10 minutes or until centres spring back when cooked.

(Read mixing/baking details on page 7)

❦ SIZE: Mini or medium muffins. ❦ TOPPINGS: Sesame seeds, pumpkin seeds ❦ SERVE: Mini muffins are good with drinks. Cut almost in half and add a slice of interesting cheese. Good for picnics. Medium muffins are good for lunch.

Leek & Bacon Muffins

Chopped leeks give muffins a pretty colour as well as a surprisingly strong flavour, which is intensified by the bacon. Replace the bacon with ham if you do not want to precook the bacon.

1½ cups self-raising flour
1 cup (100 g) grated tasty cheese
½ tsp salt
1 Tbsp sugar
pinch of cayenne pepper

½ small leek, chopped (1 cup)
2 rashers bacon, cooked
1 egg
1 cup milk

Measure the first five (dry) ingredients into a large bowl. Mix with a fork until well combined.

Cook the chopped leek in 2 tablespoons water, either in a saucepan or a microwave oven, for about 2–3 minutes until just tender, but still bright green. Chop bacon finely.

In another container beat the egg and milk together, add the cooked leek and chopped bacon, then add to the dry mixture. Without overmixing fold everything together. Flour should be dampened, the mixture should not be smooth.

Coat 12 medium sized muffin pans with Chef Mate non-stick spray. Put about ¼ cup of mixture in each muffin cup.

Bake at 210°C for 12–14 minutes, until muffins spring back when pressed.

(Read mixing/baking details on page 7).

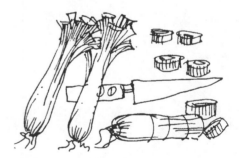

🍎 SIZE: Medium or Monster 🍎 SERVE: For lunch or a light weekend meal.

Pinenut & Pesto Muffins

These muffins are a good accompaniment to any meal which has a Mediterranean flavour. I usually bake this mixture as mini muffins. My favourite topping is cream cheese, then a little sun-dried dried tomato spread.

¼ cup pinenuts
1¼ cups self-raising flour
¾ cup (75 g) grated tasty cheese
¼ tsp salt

1 egg
¼ cup milk
2 Tbsp pesto

While the oven is heating, brown the pinenuts lightly. This should take 3–5 minutes. Put the prepared nuts in a large bowl with the flour, cheese and salt.

Beat the egg, milk and pesto together until blended.

Tip the liquid into the dry ingredients. Mix just enough to dampen dry ingredients.

Spoon into 18–24 mini-muffin pans which have been sprayed with Chef Mate non-stick spray. Bake at 200°C for about 12 minutes, until the centres spring back when pressed.

(Read mixing/baking details on page 7)

❦ SIZE: Best as mini, may be medium. ❦ SERVE: With Mediterranean-style vegetable dishes, barbecues, or pass with drinks.

Broccoli & Blue Cheese Muffins

Blue cheese mixed with the milk in these muffins puts a definite but not strong flavour through them.

1½ cups self-raising flour
1 cup (100 g) grated tasty cheese
½ tsp oreganum
½ tsp garlic salt
2 spring onions, chopped
pinch sugar

1 egg
1 cup milk
¼ cup (30 g) blue cheese
100 grams broccoli

Measure the flour into a large bowl, add the cheese. Crumble the oreganum and add with the garlic salt, spring onions and sugar. Mix well to combine. In another bowl, or using a food processor, beat together the egg, milk and blue cheese until smooth.

Prepare the broccoli by cutting it into tiny florets and peeling stems. Blanch in boiling water or microwave for 1 minute on High (100%) Power. Refresh with cold running water and drain well.

Add the broccoli to the egg, milk mixture and taking care not to overmix, add to dry ingredients.

Coat muffin pans with Chef Mate non-stick spray. Place spoonfuls of mixture into muffin pans.

Bake at 210°C for 12–15 minutes, until muffins spring back when pressed in the middle.

(Read mixing/baking details on page 7).

VARIATION:
Make these without broccoli for fingerfood for parties.

❧ SIZE: Mini, Medium or Monster ❧ SERVE: Warm, with coffee, for lunch, with soup, and at parties with drinks.

Mushroom & Ham Muffins

These muffins make a good lunch, especially if you have a leafy salad with them.

1½ cups self-raising flour
1 cup (100 g) grated tasty cheese
½ cup (75 g) ham, finely chopped
½ tsp garlic salt
1 Tbsp sugar
pinch of cayenne pepper

25 grams butter
2 cups (100 g) finely chopped
    mushrooms
1 spring onion, finely chopped
1 tsp fresh thyme, finely chopped
1 egg
1 cup milk

Measure the self-raising flour, grated cheese, ham, garlic salt, sugar and cayenne pepper into a large bowl. Mix with your fingertips to combine.

Heat the butter in a medium sized frying pan and cook the mushrooms, spring onion and thyme over a medium heat, until the mushrooms have softened.

Beat the egg and milk together, add the mushroom mixture and mix well. Pour over the dry ingredients and fold the two mixtures together taking care not to over mix.

Spray 12 medium sized muffin pans with Chef Mate non-stick spray. Put about ¼ cup of the mixture in each muffin cup.

Bake at 210°C for 12–15 minutes, until muffins spring back when pressed.

(Read mixing/baking details on page 7)

❧ SIZE: Mini, Medium or Monster ❧ SERVE: As fingerfood with drinks, as the main part of lunch, with soup or a salad.

Sizzled Sausage & Sage Muffins

"Stretch" a small amount of plain sausagemeat to feed a crowd or use your favourite "Gourmet" sausages, (skinned) in an interesting and different way. Change the herb to suit your sausage, trying, for example, chopped frankfurters and fresh fennel!

1½ cups self-raising flour
1 cup (100 g) grated tasty cheese
¼ cup chopped parsley
½ tsp salt
1 tsp sugar
pinch of cayenne pepper

2 Tbsp oil
1 onion, chopped finely
250–350 grams sausage meat
2 Tbsp finely chopped fresh sage or
*   1 tsp dried sage, crumbled*
1 egg
1 cup milk

Measure the first six ingredients into a fairly large bowl. Toss with a fork to mix.

Heat the oil in a medium-sized frypan. Add the chopped onion and the sausage meat and break it into small pieces as it cooks, until browned. Blot off any fat with a paper towel, then stir in the sage and cool.

In another container, beat the egg and milk together. Pour this over the dry ingredients, with the cooled sausage mixture. Stir only enough to combine.

Coat 12 medium sized muffin pans with Chef Mate non-stick spray. Put about ¼ cup of mixture in each muffin cup.

Optional topping: Sprinkle each muffin with a little extra grated cheese and paprika or chili powder.

Bake at 210°C for 12–15 minutes, until muffins spring back when pressed.

(Read mixing/baking details on page 7)

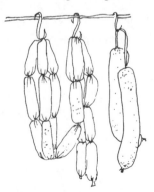

🍎 SIZE: Mini, Medium or Monster 🍎 SERVE: As fingerfood, or as the main part of lunch, or a light evening meal.

Banana Bran Muffins

Fruit Salad Muffins

Onion & Apple Muffins

These muffins have an interesting flavour which many people associate with stuffing. They go well at a barbecue with sausages or other grilled meat, but are rather nice when made as Mini muffins, with (unstuffed) roast poultry.

2 cups self-raising flour
1 cup (100 g) grated tasty cheese
1 Tbsp sugar
1 tsp salt
pinch chili powder

2 small onions
50 grams butter
1 apple, grated
2 tsp fresh thyme, finely chopped
1 egg
1¼ cups milk

Measure the first five (dry) ingredients into a large bowl, toss well to combine.

Chop the onions finely. Heat the butter in a small frying pan and cook the chopped onion until golden brown. Add the grated apple and thyme and cook until the apple has browned slightly. Cool.

In another bowl, beat the egg and milk until well mixed. Add the onion and apple mixture and tip over the dry ingredients. Taking care not to over-mix, fold everything together, until flour is barely dampened.

Coat 12 medium sized muffin pans with Chef Mate non-stick spray. Put about ¼ cup of mixture into each muffin pan.

Bake at 200°C for 12 minutes, until muffins spring back when pressed.

(Read mixing/baking details on page 7).

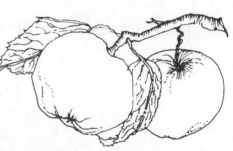

❧ SIZE: Mini, Medium or Monster ❧ SERVE: With barbecues and as bread with dinner, eg. with roast chicken.

Parmesan & Corn Muffins

These muffins contain very little fat, but still have a good flavour and texture.

1½ cups self-raising flour
2 Tbsp grated Parmesan cheese
½ tsp salt
freshly ground black pepper

440g can whole kernel corn
about ½ cup milk
2 eggs
2 spring onions, chopped

Sieve flour into a large bowl. Add Parmesan cheese, salt and pepper to taste. Toss to mix.

Drain the corn, saving the liquid, and make it up to 1 cup with milk. Beat the eggs, add drained corn, corn liquid/milk mixture and spring onion. Stir to combine.

Fold into the dry mixture, taking care not to over-mix.

Coat 9–12 medium muffin pans with Chef Mate non-stick spray. Spoon the mixture into prepared pans and sprinkle with a little paprika.

Bake at 200°C for 14–16 minutes, until muffins spring back when pressed in the middle.

(Read mixing/baking details on page 7).

❦ SIZE: Mini or Medium ❦ SERVE: As fingerfood with drinks, for lunch and for picnics.

Golden Cornmeal Muffins

These muffins make a good summer lunch, especially when served outdoors with salads. I love the
slight grittiness which cornmeal gives them. (Do not use very fine, flour-like cornmeal for this recipe).

1 cup white or wholemeal flour
½ cup yellow cornmeal
3 tsp baking powder
1 cup (100 g) grated tasty cheese
¼ cup sugar
¼ tsp salt

50 grams butter
1 egg
½ cup creamed corn
½ cup yoghurt or milk

Measure the flour, cornmeal, baking powder, cheese, sugar and salt into a large mixing bowl. Toss well with a fork.

In another container, melt the butter. Add the egg and creamed corn and mix with a fork. Add plain yoghurt in preference to milk — it makes muffins more tender.

Fold the liquid mixture into the dry ingredients, taking great care not to overmix.

Coat 12 medium-sized muffin pans with Chef Mate non-stick spray. Put about ¼ cup of mixture in each muffin cup.

Bake at 210°C for 10–15 minutes, until quite crusty and nicely browned.

(Read mixing/baking details on page 7).

picnic pleasures

❦ SIZE: Mini or Medium ❦ SERVE: Warm as fingerfood at parties, or serve for lunch, as part of a buffet, or as picnic food.

Californian Cornbread Muffins

Where but California would you find muffins flavoured with currants, orange peel, honey, corn, garlic and coriander leaves? Having said this, I must also say that I like the resulting, rather odd combination of flavours. They go well with barbecued meat and salad.

1¼ cups (gritty) yellow cornmeal
½ cup flour
2 tsp baking powder
1 tsp salt
½ cup currants
about ¼ cup finely chopped
    coriander leaves

2 cloves garlic, finely chopped
75g butter melted
¼ cup honey
1 tsp grated orange or tangelo rind
3 eggs
½ cup whole kernel corn
½ cup milk

Measure the cornmeal, flour, baking powder and salt into a large bowl and stir to mix thoroughly. Add the currants and the finely chopped coriander leaves and mix again.

Chop the garlic finely and heat with the butter in another container until butter melts. Measure the honey with a hot wet container, so that it does not stick, then add it to the butter with the orange rind, and warm until well mixed. Add the eggs and beat in thoroughly with a fork. Stir in the drained corn and the milk.

Pour the liquid mixture into the dry ingredients, and mix just enough to combine.

Using a quarter cup measure, divide the fairly wet mixture evenly between 12 medium muffin cups which have been sprayed with Chef Mate non-stick spray.

Bake at 200°C until centres feel firm when pressed, about 12 minutes.

(Read baking/mixing details on page 7).

❦ SIZE: Medium or Mini ❦ SERVE: Freshly made as an accompaniment to barbecued or grilled meats.

Basic Bran Muffins

These bran muffins are very easy and quick to make. Because they have no added butter or oil they stick easily, prepare the muffin pans carefully. Spread with cottage cheese or quark and top with red currant or crabapple jelly, for a real treat!

2 cups wheat bran
½ cup flour
1 tsp baking powder
1 tsp baking soda
½ cup sultanas, optional
¼ cup chopped walnuts, optional

½ cup golden syrup or treacle
1 egg
1 cup milk

Put the bran into a large mixing bowl, sieve onto the bran the next three dry ingredients. Add the sultanas and/or walnuts if you are using them then mix everything together lightly, with your fingers.

Warm the golden syrup or treacle in a saucepan or microwave bowl until runny. Remove from the heat, then add the egg and milk and mix well. Pour the liquids onto the dry ingredients and fold together only until the dry ingredients are barely dampened.

Divide the mixture evenly between 12 medium-sized muffin pans that have been well coated with Chef Mate non-stick spray.

Bake at 200°C for about 10–15 minutes or until firm in the middle when pressed lightly.

(Read mixing/baking details on page 7)

🍎 SIZE: Medium and mini 🍎 SERVE: For brunch, with tea or coffee or at any time of the day. Excellent in packed lunches.

Fruited Honey Muffins

These muffins will fill the kitchen with a lovely smell as they cook because of the malty Allbran in them.

½ cup Allbran
¼ cup boiling water

¾ cup flour
¾ cup wheat bran
½ tsp baking soda
2 Tbsp sugar

100 grams butter
2 Tbsp honey
1 egg
½ cup yoghurt (any flavour)
1 banana, chopped

Soak the Allbran in the boiling water, and leave to cool.

Measure the dry ingredients into a large mixing bowl and toss with a fork.

Melt the butter and honey together in the microwave or in a saucepan over low heat, just until the butter has melted and

the honey is soft enough to mix easily with the butter. Add the egg and yoghurt and beat lightly with a fork, just to combine. Stir in the chopped banana.

Add the Allbran and liquid mixtures to the dry ingredients then fold everything together taking care not to overmix.

Divide the mixture evenly between 12 medium-sized muffin pans which have been coated with Chef Mate non-stick spray.

Bake at 200°C for about 15 minutes, or until lightly browned, and firm in the middle when pressed.

(Read mixing/baking details page 7)

❦ SIZE: Medium or mini ❦ SERVE: Serve for weekend breakfasts and brunches, with tea or coffee, in children's lunches or as after-school snacks

Banana Bran Muffins

These muffins are delicious! When they are freshly made you can serve them just as they are, without butter or any other toppings, because they taste so good.

¾ cup flour
¾ cup wholemeal flour
¾ cup brown sugar
½ cup wheat bran
2 tsp baking powder
2 tsp cinnamon
½ cup chopped walnuts (optional)
½ cup sultanas (optional)

50 grams butter
1 egg
1½ cups mashed banana
1 tsp vanilla
milk, as required

In a large bowl measure all the dry ingredients. Add the chopped walnuts and sultanas. Mix thoroughly with your fingers to combine.

Melt the butter until liquid, stir in the egg, and mix well with a fork. Add the mashed banana and vanilla and mix again.

Stir the liquids into the dry ingredients and without overmixing, fold everything together. (If you use barely ripe bananas you may need to add milk until you have a mixture of normal muffin consistency.)

Divide the mixture evenly between 12 medium-sized muffin pans that have been well coated with Chef Mate non-stick spray.

Bake at 200°C for 10–15 minutes or until the centres spring back when lightly pressed.

(Read mixing/baking details page 7)

🍎 SIZE: Medium or mini 🍎 SERVE: Suitable to serve for breakfast, brunch, or lunch, or coffee, in packed lunches, and as an after-school snack.

Kiwi Bran Muffins

When you eat these muffins warm from the oven you would hardly know that they have bran in them!

2 cups self-raising flour
½ cup wheat bran
½ cup brown sugar
½ tsp baking soda
1 tsp cinnamon

50 grams butter
1 household Tbsp golden syrup
1 egg
1 cup milk

3 medium kiwifruit, cubed
¼ cup chopped walnuts

Measure the first five ingredients into a large bowl and toss to mix.

In a saucepan or microwave bowl heat the butter and golden syrup until liquid and mixable. Add egg and milk and beat with a fork to mix.

Peel and chop the kiwifruit into 7 mm cubes. Pour the liquid mixture into the dry ingredients, add the chopped kiwifruit and walnuts and fold together to combine without overmixing.

Divide mixture between 12 medium muffin pans which have been well coated with Chef Mate non-stick spray.

Bake at 200°C for 12–15 minutes, until the centres of the muffins will spring back when lightly pressed.

VARIATION:
Replace kiwifruit with 1–1½ cups of other raw cubed fruit.

(Read mixing/baking details page 7)

🍎 SIZE: Mini and medium 🍎 SERVE: For breakfast, brunch, with tea or coffee at any time, in packed lunches and as after-school snacks.

Date & Yoghurt Muffins

Dates for flavour, yoghurt for extra tenderness and bran for fibre - what more could you ask for in a muffin!
Made as mini-muffins, warm from the oven, you will probably find that these need no extra spreads.

1½ cups self-raising flour
2 cups wheat bran
1 cup brown sugar
1 tsp baking soda
1 cup dates, chopped
½ cup chopped walnuts

½ cup oil
2 eggs
1½ cups yoghurt (any flavour)

Measure the first four ingredients into a bowl and mix to combine. (Measure the baking soda into the palm of your hand and flatten with your finger to ensure that all the lumps are removed before adding to the other ingredients.) Stir in the chopped dates and walnuts.

In another bowl beat together the oil, eggs and yoghurt with a fork until smooth. Pour all the liquid into the dry ingredients then fold together until just combined.

Divide the mixture evenly between 12 medium-sized muffin pans that have been well coated with Chef Mate non-stick spray.

Bake at 200°C for about 10 minutes or until the centre will spring back when lightly pressed.

(Read the mixing/baking details page 7)

❧ SIZE: Medium or mini ❧ TOPPING: Top with Cinnamon Sugar (page 61) before baking, if desired. ❧ SERVE: For brunch, with tea or coffee at any time of the day

Banana Allbran Muffins

*Very few of the people who enjoy these muffins warm from my oven ever realise that they have bran in them!
The malty Allbran flavour goes well with the banana, but you can replace it with other fruit, if you like.*

1 cup self-raising flour
1 cup Allbran
¼ cup sugar
¼ tsp salt

grated rind of 1 orange
1 cup orange juice/milk
¼ cup oil
1 egg
1 banana

Measure the flour, Allbran, sugar and salt into a fairly large mixing bowl. Stir the ingredients well to combine.

Grate the orange rind needed, then squeeze the orange and measure the juice. In another container put the amount of milk required to bring the total quantity of liquid up to one cup.

Combine the orange juice and rind, the oil and egg and beat with a fork. Peel the banana and cut into small cubes. Add to the egg mixture. Add the egg mixture and the milk separately to the dry ingredients and fold everything together carefully until the flour is dampened, but the mixture is not smooth.

Spray 12 medium-sized muffin pans with Chef Mate non-stick spray. Put about ¼ cup of mixture in each muffin cup.

Bake at 225°C for 10–12 minutes, until muffins spring back when pressed.

(Read mixing/baking details on page 7).

❦ SIZE: Medium and mini ❦ SERVE: Warm for breakfast, with morning or afternoon coffee, as an after-school snack. Lovely spread with quark, cottage cheese and orange cream cheese.

Tutti Fruity Muffins

These low-fat muffins are always popular. They have such a good flavour they do not need buttering, as long as you eat them warm from the oven. They stale quickly, so if you are not going to eat them all the day they are made you should freeze those which are left.

2 cups flour
1 cup oat bran
1 tsp baking soda
1 tsp baking powder
1 cup brown sugar

2 eggs
¾ cup apricot or orange yoghurt
½ cup milk
¼ cup concentrated orange juice
1 banana, mashed
2 Tbsp passionfruit pulp, if
   available

Toss the flour, oat bran, baking soda and baking powder together, thoroughly, in a large mixing bowl. Add the sugar and mix again.

In another bowl, beat the eggs, yoghurt, milk and orange juice together, using a fork. Add the mashed banana and passion fruit pulp and mix again.

Tip the liquid mixture into the dry ingredients, then taking care not to overmix, fold the two together, stopping as soon as the dry ingredients are dampened.

Put spoonfuls of the mixture into 12 medium-sized muffin pans that have been well coated with Chef Mate non-stick spray.

Bake at 200°C for 10–15 minutes or until the centres spring back when pressed.

(Read mixing/baking details page 7)

❧ SIZE: Medium or mini ❧ SERVE: For breakfasts, brunches, as after-school snacks, for picnics and in packed lunches.

Bulk Bran Muffins

This recipe makes about three dozen medium-sized muffins. You can refrigerate the uncooked mixture for up to two weeks, cooking them as required. As the muffins can be microwaved, hungry children can cook their own muffins from the refrigerated mixture.

½ cup treacle
2 cups rolled oats
1 cup baking bran
1 cup boiling water
1 cup brown sugar
2 Tbsp wine vinegar
1 tsp salt
2 eggs
2 cups milk
2 cups flour
1 cup oat bran
1½ tsp baking soda

Measure the treacle, rolled oats and baking bran into a large bowl. Pour over boiling water and stir until treacle and oats are mixed. Leave to cool for 5 minutes, then add the brown sugar, vinegar, salt and eggs. Beat with a fork to combine eggs.

Add the milk and then the flour, oat bran and baking soda, previously forked together. Stir only enough to combine.

Spray muffin pans with Chef Mate non-stick spray. Put about ¼ cup of mixture in each muffin cup.

Bake at 220°C for about 10 minutes, until muffins spring back when pressed.

OR Microwave in paper cases in microwave muffin moulds, for about 2 minutes on High (100%) Power for 5 muffins. Microwave ovens vary — experiment with the first few batches you make until you know the exact time taken by your microwave oven. Always leave to stand for a few minutes before removing muffins from pans.

(Read mixing/baking details on page 7)

❧ SIZE: Medium ❧ SERVE: Warm for breakfast, brunch, with coffee, in lunches or after school. Serve microwaved muffins within 30 minutes of cooking.

Best Blueberry Muffins

Everybody likes the idea of blueberry muffins. Blueberries make good muffins because they are not sour when cooked. Use frozen free-flow blueberries when fresh ones are not available. To stop frozen blueberries staining the batter, use them before they thaw completely.

2 cups flour
4 tsp baking powder
1 tsp cinnamon
½ tsp salt
½ cup caster sugar

100 grams butter
1 cup milk
1 egg
1–1½ cups blueberries

Sieve the first five (dry) ingredients into a fairly large bowl.

In another container warm butter until melted, then add the milk and egg, and beat to mix thoroughly.

Prepare fresh or partly frozen berries, then tip the liquid and fruit into the bowl with the dry mixture. Without overmixing, fold everything together. Flour should be dampened, not smooth. Berries should keep their shape.

Divide the mixture evenly between 12 medium-sized muffin pans that have been well coated with Chef Mate non-stick spray. Top with Cinnamon Sugar or make Streusel Topping, (page 61).

Bake at 220°C for 12–15 minutes, until muffins spring back when pressed. (Muffins made with frozen berries will take about 5 minutes longer.)

(Read mixing/baking details on page 7)

❦ SIZE: Mini or Medium ❦ SERVE: always warm, for breakfast, with coffee, for lunch, for dessert.

Carrot & Walnut Muffins

If you like the flavour of Hotcross Buns but don't have the time to make them, try these spicy muffins instead. Don't save them only for Easter celebrations though - they taste good at any time.

¾ cup flour
½ tsp salt
½ tsp baking soda
2 tsp cinnamon
1 tsp ground allspice
¾ cup brown sugar
¼ cup chopped walnuts
½ cup sultanas

½ cup oil
2 eggs
200g carrots, grated

Sieve the first 5 ingredients into a large bowl. Add brown sugar, walnuts and sultanas and mix these evenly through the dry ingredients with your fingers, breaking up any lumps.

In another bowl beat the oil and eggs together and add the finely grated carrot.

Tip the oil and egg mixture into the dry mixture. Taking care not to overmix, fold everything together until there are no more unmixed lumps of flour.

Spray 12 medium-sized muffin pans with Chef Mate non-stick spray. Put about ¼ cup of mixture into each pan.

Bake at 190°C for about 15 minutes, or until the centre of the muffins spring back when pressed.

(Read mixing/baking details on page 7).

❧ SIZE: Mini or Medium ❧ SERVE: Warm with coffee. Nice for dessert, split, with Rum Butter (see page 61).

Banana Blueberry Muffins

*Freeze blueberries when they are in season so you can make these
popular muffins all year round.*

2 cups flour
2 tsp baking powder
¼ tsp baking soda
½ cup caster sugar

50 grams butter
½ cup milk
1 orange, grated rind and ½ cup
    juice
2 eggs
½ tsp vanilla
1 large ripe banana
1 cup blueberries, fresh or frozen

3 Tbsp Cinnamon Sugar
    (see page 61).

Sieve flour, baking powder, baking soda and caster sugar together into a large bowl.

In another container, warm the butter until it has melted. Remove from the heat and beat in the milk, orange rind and juice, eggs and vanilla. Mash the banana and stir into the liquid mixture with the blueberries. Tip this mixture onto the dry ingredients and fold together until dry ingredients are barely damp.

Spray 12 medium-sized muffin pans with Chef Mate non-stick spray. Put about ¼ cup of mixture in each muffin cup. Sprinkle with Cinnamon Sugar.

Bake at 200°C for 10–12 minutes or until muffins spring back when pressed in the centre.

(Read mixing/baking details on page 7).

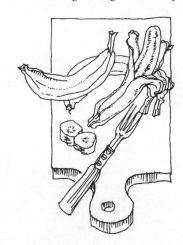

❧ SIZE: Medium ❧ SERVE: Warm, for brunch, with coffee, for lunch and dessert.

Spicy Pineapple Muffins

These muffins are deliciously spicy. The quantity of mixed spice really is one tablespoon, but remember to use a level measuring tablespoon, or your muffins and mine won't be the same.

2 cups flour
1 Tbsp mixed spice
1 tsp baking soda
½ cup sugar
¼ tsp salt
1 cup sultanas

100 grams butter
2 eggs
450 gram can crushed pineapple

Sieve, into a large bowl the flour, mixed spice, baking soda, sugar and salt. Add the sultanas and toss with the flour mixture to combine.

In another container, melt the butter. Add the eggs and beat well. Drain the pineapple through a sieve, push with a spoon to extract as much liquid as possible. Measure the drained pineapple you should have about 1 cup of fruit and ¾ cup juice. Add the measured fruit and juice to the egg mixture. Pour over the mixed dry ingredients. Fold everything together until the flour has been dampened, but the mixture looks lumpy and under-mixed.

Spray 12 medium sized muffin pans with Chef Mate non-stick spray. Put about ¼ cup of mixture in each muffin cup.

Bake at 200°C for 10–15 minutes, until muffins spring back when pressed in the centre.

(Read mixing/baking details on page 7).

🍍 SIZE: Medium 🍍 SERVE: Warm with morning or afternoon tea, in a packed lunch, or when it is your turn to "bring a plate". For "Special Caribbean Muffins" serve warm for dessert with Rum Butter (see page 61.)

Best Blueberry Muffins

Chocolate & Banana Muffins

Spiced Apple Muffins

Make these muffins only after you know what consistency a muffin mixture should be. Raw apple gives muffins a lovely fresh apple flavour, but when you use it, you never know exactly how much milk will be needed.

1 cup self-raising flour
1 cup (fine) rolled oats
¾ cup brown sugar
2 tsp mixed spice
2 tsp cinnamon
½ tsp ground cloves
½ tsp baking soda
½ tsp salt

75 grams butter
1 egg
1 cup raw chopped or grated apple
¾ –1 cup milk

Measure the dry ingredients into a large mixing bowl and mix well with your fingers to ensure that the rolled oats and brown sugar are mixed evenly through the other ingredients.

Melt the butter until liquid then add the egg and ¾ cup of the milk, and beat with a fork until mixed. Next, grate or chop the apple in a food processor. Press it into the cup, removing air bubbles, then stir it into the liquids. (Work quickly to prevent the apple browning.)

Add the apple and liquid mixture to the dry ingredients and mix lightly to dampen the ingredients, adding as much of the extra ¼ cup of milk as you need.

Coat 12 medium-sized muffin pans with Chef Mate non-stick spray and divide the mixture between them.

Bake at 200°C for 12–15 minutes or until the muffins spring back when pressed. Leave for 3–4 minutes before removing from the pans and cooling on a wire rack.

(Read mixing/baking details page 7)

🍂 SIZE: Medium or mini 🍂 SERVE: For morning tea or brunch. Nice in packed lunches and popular as after-school snacks.

Sweet Spicy Pumpkin Muffins

*Muffins are easily mixed and make marvellous after-school snacks. Teach
your teenagers how easy it is to make them for themselves!*

2 cups self-raising flour
1½ cups brown sugar
½ tsp baking soda
1 tsp cinnamon
½ tsp grated nutmeg
½ tsp ground ginger
¼ tsp ground cloves

100 grams butter
2 eggs
1 cup cooked, mashed pumpkin

Measure the first 7 (dry) ingredients into a large bowl. Toss with a fork to combine thoroughly.

In another container, warm the butter until melted, add the eggs and beat well. Stir in the mashed pumpkin. Add to the dry mixture and fold together without over-mixing.

Spray 12 medium muffin pans with Chef Mate non-stick spray. Put about ¼ cup of the mixture in each muffin cup.

Bake at 200°C for 15–18 minutes until golden brown and until they spring back when pressed in the centre.

(Read mixing/baking details on page 7)

NOTE:
Cook cubed pumpkin until tender, in a microwave oven, then mash with a fork. It is best not to use buttered, peppered purée or pumpkin which is overcooked, dark coloured and soggy.

❦ SIZE: Mini or Medium ❦ SERVE: Warm, with coffee for lunch. Good after school. Nice for dessert, with Rum Butter (see page 61) or split, with whipped cream and fresh fruit.

Double Chocolate Muffins

This recipe will delight chocolate lovers! You may think that the chocolate chips on the top of a chocolate muffin may be gilding the lily, but they provide an interesting texture as well as giving a stronger flavour.

1¾ cups flour
1 tsp baking soda
1 cup caster sugar
¼ cup cocoa

100 grams butter
1 egg
1 cup yoghurt
½ cup milk
½ tsp vanilla

¼–½ cup chocolate chips

Sift the dry ingredients into a large mixing bowl.

Melt the butter, add the remaining ingredients and mix until smooth.

Add the combined liquids to the dry ingredients and fold together until the flour is dampened, but not smooth.

Divide the mixture evenly between 12 medium-sized muffin pans that have been well coated with Chef Mate non-stick spray.

Sprinkle with chocolate chips if desired before baking.

Bake at 200°C for 10–12 minutes or until centres spring back when pressed lightly. Leave to stand in the pans for about 3 minutes before removing and cooling on a wire rack.

(Read mixing/baking details page 7)

❦ SIZE: Mini or medium ❦ SERVE: With coffee for lunch. Make mini muffins for children's parties. Split muffins and serve for dessert with fresh strawberries or with raspberry jam and whipped cream.

Fruit Salad Muffins

When you want to brighten a winter's day and you don't have fresh fruit on hand, drain a can of fruit
salad and use it, and some of the juice from it, to make these fruit salad muffins!

2 cups flour
4 tsp baking powder
½ cup sugar
½ tsp salt

425 gram can Fruit Salad
75 grams butter
½ cup milk
1 egg

Sift together the flour, baking powder, sugar and salt into a large mixing bowl.

Drain the juice from the can of fruit salad, measure ¼ cup of this juice and add to the melted butter with the milk and egg. Beat with a whisk or fork to combine.

Cut any large pieces of fruit (and the cherries) into smaller pieces and add to the sifted dry ingredients with the liquids. Mix briefly, until mixtures are just combined.

Coat 12 medium sized muffin pans with Chef Mate non-stick spray and spoon about ¼ cup of the mixture into each pan.

OPTIONAL :
Sprinkle with Cinnamon Sugar (see page 61).

Bake at 200°C for 10–12 minutes or until the centres spring back when pressed.

(Read mixing/baking details page 7)

❦ SIZE: Mini or medium ❦ SERVE: For weekend brunch, with tea or coffee or for dessert.

Chocolate & Banana Muffins

Here is a recipe which is well worth trying. The banana flavour is strongest when you use over-ripe bananas. If you do not like the idea of pieces of chocolate in muffins, replace the chocolate with half the amount of chopped walnuts.

2 cups self-raising flour
½ cup caster sugar
½ cup chocolate chips
½ tsp salt

100 grams butter
1 cup milk
1 egg
1 tsp vanilla essence
1 cup (2–3) mashed bananas

With a fork, stir together in a large bowl the flour, caster sugar, chocolate chips and salt.

In another container, melt the butter, remove from the heat, then add the milk, egg and vanilla and beat well.

Mash and measure the bananas and stir them into the liquid. Tip all the liquid mixture into the bowl with the dry mixture. Fold everything together carefully until all the flour is dampened, stopping before the mixture is smooth.

Spray 12 medium muffin pans with Chef Mate non-stick spray. Put about ¼ cup of mixture into each cup.

Bake at 220°C for 12–15 minutes, until muffins spring back when pressed in the centre.

(Read mixing/baking details page 7).

🌱 **SIZE:** Medium and Mini. 🌱 **SERVE:** Mini Muffins make very popular snacks for young children, and are good for lunch boxes and after-school snacks. Serve with tea or coffee at any time of the day. Dare I mention it - these are delicious with Rum Butter, too!

Orange Honey Muffins

These muffins have a good flavour and are beautifully moist and tender.

2 cups flour
4 tsp baking powder
¼ cup sugar
grated rind of 2 oranges

75 grams butter
¼ cup honey
1 egg
¾ cup orange juice/milk

Measure the flour, baking powder, sugar and orange rind into a fairly large bowl. Toss lightly with a fork to mix thoroughly.

In another container melt the butter. Add the honey and heat again. Use as little heat as is necessary. Break the egg into the mixture, and beat with a fork to mix. Squeeze the oranges and measure the volume of juice. Without mixing the liquids, measure enough milk to make the total volume up to ¾ cup. Stir the orange juice into the melted butter mixture. Pour the melted butter mixture over the dry ingredients.

Fold the two mixtures together. When they are partly combined, add the milk. Stir again, stopping as soon as you can see no unmixed flour. Do not mix until smooth.

Spray 12 medium muffin pans with Chef Mate non-stick spray. Put about ¼ cup of mixture into each muffin cup.

Bake at 200° C for 10–12 minutes, or until the centres spring back when pressed.

(Read mixing/baking details on page 7)

❧ SIZE: Mini or Medium ❧ SERVE: Warm for a weekend breakfast, with tea or coffee for a mid-morning or mid-afternoon break, include in a packed lunch, good for after-school snacks.

Crunchy Lemon Muffins

Everybody at our house rates these muffins VERY highly! The sugar and lemon juice drizzled over the top, after baking, gives a tangy flavour and an interesting sugary crunch.

2 cups self-raising flour
¾ cup sugar

75 grams butter
1 cup milk
1 egg
grated rind of 1 large or 2 small lemons

¼ cup lemon juice
¼ cup sugar

Measure the flour and sugar into a bowl and toss to mix.

Melt the butter, add the milk, egg and lemon rind and beat well with a fork to combine. Add the liquids to the dry ingredients and combine only until the dry ingredients have been lightly dampened but not thoroughly mixed.

Divide the mixture evenly between 12 medium-sized muffin pans that have been well coated with Chef Mate non-stick spray.

Bake at 200°C for 10 minutes.

(Read mixing/baking details on page 7)

Stir together the lemon juice and sugar without dissolving the sugar, and drizzle this over the hot muffins as soon as they are removed from the oven. Leave to stand in the pans only for a few minutes after this, in case the syrup hardens as it cools and sticks the muffins to the pans. If this happens, it may be necessary to use a knife to "lever" the muffins from the pan. Take care not to damage the pan's non-stick finish.

🍎 SIZE: Medium 🍎 SERVE: With tea or coffee for afternoon tea or as a dessert served with lightly whipped cream and fresh fruit or berries.

Ginger Cardamom Muffins

*This is the same basic recipe that my mother used to make her delicious ginger gems. I add cardamom to
these as well as ginger, because I love the aromatic flavour, but leave it out if you don't like this spice!*

2 cups flour
1 tsp baking soda
1 cup caster sugar
2 tsp ground ginger
1 tsp ground cardamom, optional

2 heaped household Tbsp golden
    syrup
100 grams butter
2 eggs
1 cup milk

In a large bowl mix together the dry ingredients.

In a microwave dish or a saucepan on the stove, warm together the butter and golden syrup until the butter has just melted and the syrup is warm. Remove from the heat and leave to cool slightly before adding the eggs and milk. Beat well to combine all the liquid ingredients.

Without overmixing add the liquids to the dry ingredients and lightly mix.

Coat 12-15 medium muffin pans with Chef Mate non-stick spray or if cooking in gem irons, heat the gem irons at 200°C until very hot. Spray these with Chef Mate non-stick spray and spoon the mixture from the side of a tablespoon into the hot irons so each is about ⅔ full.

Bake gems at 200°C for about
12 minutes or until the centres spring back when pressed. Leave 2–3 minutes then remove from the pans or irons. Bake muffins a little longer, testing them the same way before removing from the oven.

(Read mixing/baking instructions page 7)

❧ SIZE: Mini and Medium ❧ SERVE: For lunch or afternoon tea. Nice for a dessert, with Rum Butter or whipped cream and fresh fruit.

Leek & Bacon Mini-Muffins • Best Blueberry Mini-Muffins • Spicy Pineapple Mini-Muffins

Orange & Honey Muffins

Apricot & Walnut Muffins

Dried fruits and nuts always make good additions to muffins! If you can find New Zealand dried apricots, use them in this recipe, they give an extra-strong apricot flavour to the mixture, since they break up after being heated in the water or juice.

2 cups flour
1 tsp baking soda
1 cup brown sugar
1 tsp cinnamon

½ cup chopped dried apricots
¼ cup water or orange juice

100 grams butter
2 eggs
1 cup yoghurt
1 large orange, rind and juice
½ cup chopped walnuts

Measure the dry ingredients into a large bowl and mix well to ensure that brown sugar is evenly mixed through the other ingredients.

In another bowl microwave the apricots with the water or juice until all the liquid is absorbed (about 1 minute on High [100%] Power).

Add the butter, warming again if necessary, then mix in the eggs and yoghurt, and the grated rind. Make the juice from the orange up to ½ cup with water, if necessary, and add this and the chopped walnuts.

Fold the two mixtures together, taking care not to overmix.

Divide the mixture evenly between 12 medium-sized muffin pans that have been well coated with Chef Mate non-stick spray.

Bake at 190°C for about 12–15 minutes or until the muffins spring back when pressed lightly.

(Read mixing/baking details on page 7)

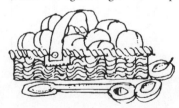

❧ SIZE: Medium and Mini ❧ SERVE: For a weekend brunch, with coffee any time.
Good in packed lunches, for after-school snacks and for picnics.

Strawberry Cream Cheese Muffins

The lovely strawberry flavour of these muffins reminds you of a summer day, even in mid-winter. This is a good way to use frozen strawberries, or to make a few ripe fresh berries go a long way. Use berries with a strong flavour.

2 cups self-raising flour
¾ cup sugar
¼ tsp salt

½ cup cream cheese
1 cup milk
1 egg
1 tsp finely grated orange rind
1 cup (125 g) frozen or fresh
*   strawberries chopped*

Measure the dry ingredients into a large bowl. Whisk to mix.

Measure the cream cheese into a bowl then beat until smooth, warming it if necessary. Add the milk, egg, and orange rind and combine with a whisk or beater.

Chop the frozen berries into more or less 5 mm cubes, without thawing them. Chop fresh berries into pieces the same size.

Combine the three mixtures, stirring as little as possible. Divide mixture between 12 medium muffin pans, sprayed with

Chef Mate non-stick spray, putting about ¼ cup of mixture in each.

Bake at 200°C for about 12 minutes for fresh berry muffins, and for about 15 minutes for frozen berry muffins, until centres spring back when pressed.

(Read mixing/baking details on page 7)

❦ SIZE: Mini or Medium ❦ GARNISH: Dust with icing sugar, or halve and serve with Orange Cream Cheese (page 61) and more berries, or halve and serve with ice-cream. ❦ SERVE: For afternoon tea or dessert.

Rich Raspberry Muffins

These muffins combine the flavours of raspberries and spices. You will find the same popular ingredients in Belgium biscuits and in Linzer Torte - but it takes a long time to prepare these. Do it the easy way - enjoy the same flavours in quickly-made muffins!

2 cups self-raising flour
½ cup sugar
1 tsp cinnamon
¼ tsp ground cloves

100 grams butter
1 egg
1 cup milk
1 tsp instant coffee
rind of 1 lemon
½ cup raspberry jam

¼ cup sifted icing sugar
1 – 2 tsp lemon juice

Sift the dry ingredients into a large bowl.

In another container melt the butter, add the egg and the milk in which the coffee has been dissolved. Add the lemon rind and mix well to combine.

Add the liquids to the dry ingredients and fold together without overmixing.

Coat 12 medium-sized muffin pans with Chef Mate non-stick spray and half fill each pan with the mixture. Put 2 teaspoons of raspberry jam on top of this mixture then divide the remaining mixture evenly between the pans to cover the jam filling.

Bake at 200°C for 10–12 minutes or until the centre springs back when lightly pressed.

Before muffins cool completely, drizzle with a small amount of the icing.

For icing: Put sifted icing sugar in a small bowl and add just enough lemon juice to mix to the consistency of thin cream.

(Read mixing/baking details on page 7)

❧ SIZE: Medium ❧ SERVE: With tea, coffee or for dessert

Apricot Surprise Muffins

These muffins are a favourite of mine. When you bite into them, you find a delicious mixture of dried apricots and almonds hidden in the middle. Make them for special occasions or for your best friends - but make sure you keep some for yourself!

1¾ cups self-raising flour
¾ cup sugar
¼ tsp baking soda
½ tsp salt

½ cup sour cream
½ cup milk
1 egg
½ tsp almond essence

40 grams dried apricots
½ cup water
2 Tbsp ground almonds
2 Tbsp sugar
2 Tbsp wine biscuit crumbs

Measure the first 4 (dry) ingredients into a large bowl. Mix thoroughly.

In another container, beat together the sour cream, milk, egg and almond essence. Tip the mixture into the bowl with the dry mixture. Without over-mixing, fold everything together.

To make the filling: Chop the apricots into small pieces. Boil them with the water for 3–4 minutes, until the water has disappeared. Cool, and mix with ground almonds, sugar and biscuit crumbs.

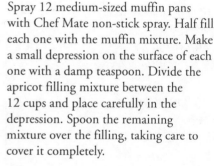

Spray 12 medium-sized muffin pans with Chef Mate non-stick spray. Half fill each one with the muffin mixture. Make a small depression on the surface of each one with a damp teaspoon. Divide the apricot filling mixture between the 12 cups and place carefully in the depression. Spoon the remaining mixture over the filling, taking care to cover it completely.

OPTIONAL:
Sprinkle with Struesel Topping (see page 61).

Bake at 200°C for 12–15 minutes, until muffins spring back when pressed.

(Read mixing/baking details on page 7).

❦ SIZE: Medium ❦ SERVE: Warm with coffee, or with whipped cream as a dessert.

Rum and Raisin Muffins

I make these muffins for a cold weather treat. If I am going to serve them with coffee, I top them with a glaze flavoured with rum essence. If they are for dessert, or for supper, I reheat them in the microwave and serve them with delicious Rum Butter - try it!

1 cup dark Californian raisins
2 Tbsp rum

2 cups flour
1½ tsp baking soda
2 tsp cinnamon
2 tsp mixed spice
¼ tsp ground cloves
¾ cup sugar
½ cup chopped walnuts

75 grams butter
1 egg
1 cup yoghurt
¾ cup milk

Put the raisins and rum into a small plastic bag. Knead bag gently. Leave to stand in a warm place while you mix the other ingredients.

Sieve the flour, soda and spices into a large bowl. Add the sugar and chopped walnuts and stir to mix thoroughly.

Melt the butter in a pot or microwave dish. Add the egg, yoghurt (any flavour) and milk. Add the marinated raisins with any remaining liquid and mix well. Now combine the liquid and dry mixtures without over-beating.

Divide the mixture evenly between 12 medium-sized muffin pans that have been well coated with Chef Mate non-stick spray.

Bake at 210°C for about 12 minutes or until centres spring back.

(Read mixing/baking details on Page 7).

☙ SIZE: Medium and/or Mini-sized muffins. ☙ SERVE for holiday season brunches, with coffee in mid-winter, or for dessert on any occasion. Top with Cinnamon Sugar (see page 61) before cooking OR Mix ¼ cup icing sugar with ½ teaspoon rum essence and about 1 tsp milk - enough to make a thin icing. Drizzle, in a thin stream, over warm muffins on rack OR Serve warm, halved, with Rum Butter (see page 61).

Cranberry Orange Muffins

What about starting a new tradition in your family? Pass these round while presents are being opened on Christmas morning OR celebrate the shortest day with mulled wine and some of these muffins.

2 cups self-raising flour
½ cup brown sugar

454 gram can Whole Berry Cranberry Sauce
¼ cup orange juice
75 grams butter
grated rind of 1 orange
2 eggs

In a large bowl, mix together thoroughly the flour and brown sugar.

In a small saucepan or in a microwave oven, warm the cranberries and orange juice until the syrup has thinned enough to strain. Sieve, without mashing the fruit, but bang sieve on the side of the bowl to extract all of the juice.

In another container, melt the butter, add strained juice, grated orange rind and eggs, beat well. Pour over flour and sugar mixture. Fold together, taking great care not to over-mix.

Spray 12 medium muffin pans with Chef Mate non-stick spray. Half fill each cup with the muffin mixture, make a depression in this with the back of a dampened teaspoon, spoon whole, drained cranberries into this, then top with remaining batter. Bake at 200°C for 12–15 minutes until muffins spring back when pressed.

(Read mixing/baking details on page 7.)

VARIATIONS:
Top with Struesel Topping (see page 61) before baking OR stir together ¼ cup of orange juice and ¼ cup of sugar, without dissolving the sugar and pour this mixture over very hot muffins (removed from the pan).

❦ SIZE: Medium ❦ SERVE: On Christmas morning, for brunch, with coffee, or for dessert, with whipped cream or rich ice-cream.

Christmas Mincemeat Muffins

Although mince pies are nice, making their crust is quite time consuming especially when there are other Christmas chores waiting. Why not put spoonfuls of mixture in muffins instead. Serve these warm, and wait for the compliments!

1¾ cups self-raising flour
¾ cup caster sugar
½ tsp salt

2 eggs
½ cup sour cream
½ cup milk
½ tsp rum, whisky or brandy
*   essence*
½ cup Christmas (fruit)
*   mincemeat*

Measure the first three ingredients into a large bowl.

In another bowl mix together with a whisk, until smooth, the eggs, sour cream, milk and essence of your choice.

Without overmixing add the liquids to the dry ingredients.

Coat 12 medium sized muffin pans with Chef Mate non-stick spray and half fill the 12 pans with the mixture. Using a dampened teaspoon, make a small indentation on the top of each, and into it put 1-2 teaspoons of the mincemeat.

Cover each with a spoonful of the remaining mixture trying to cover the "enclosed" mincemeat.

Bake at 200°C for about 12-15 minutes or until golden brown. The centres should spring back when pressed.

(Read mixing/baking details page 7)

❦ SIZE: Medium ❦ SERVE: Always warm, for Christmas Day breakfast or brunch, or with coffee at any time of the day over the holiday period. Serve hot for dessert between Christmas and New Year with fresh berries and icecream or whipped cream or with Rum or Brandy Butters (see page 61).

Marvellous toppings for muffins

Add interest to your muffins by using interesting toppings and spreads on them.

Toppings for savoury muffins

Before cooking: Add grated cheese, cubes of cheese, shreds of Parmesan, toasted sesame seeds, poppy seeds, pumpkin seeds, sunflower seeds, paprika, cayenne and chili powder on savoury muffins.

After cooking: Split muffins (sometimes from top to bottom, at other times from side to side) and use interesting spreads.

BUY: Cream cheese, cottage cheese, savoury cottage cheese, quark, butter.

MAKE: Horseradish cream cheese, herb butters, Liptauer cheese, mashed avocado.

AT TIMES: Sandwich the two halves of mini muffins, or top halved medium muffins with thin slices of ham, pastrami, smoked pork, beef or lamb, smoked salmon, mussels, luncheon sausage etc., depending on the occasion. Add sliced tomatoes, cucumber pickles, salad vegetables, etc.

HORSERADISH CREAM CHEESE
Mix together ¼ cup cream cheese and 1 Tbsp (bottled) grated horseradish or fresh grated horseradish to taste.

HERB BUTTER
Food process or mix 100 grams softened butter and ½–1 cup of chopped fresh herbs. Add ¼–½ cup finely grated Parmesan cheese if you like.

Toppings for sweet and bran-plus muffins

Before cooking: Top with cinnamon sugar, streusel topping, sesame sugar, chopped walnuts, almonds, or cashews, sunflower, pumpkin, poppy or sesame seeds, chocolate chips.

After cooking: Split muffins, and buy toppings, both as for savoury muffins.

MAKE: Orange Cream Cheese, Creamy Honey Spread, Nutty Cream Spread, Rum Butter (Alison's favourite!), Brandy Butter, or Icing to Drizzle. Sprinkle icing with slivered almonds, chopped cherries, or, for children, hundreds and thousands.

Marvellous toppings for sweet muffins

CINNAMON SUGAR
Shake together in a screw-topped jar $\frac{1}{4}$ cup of brown sugar, $\frac{1}{4}$ cup of white sugar, and 1 tablespoon of cinnamon. Sprinkle $\frac{1}{2}$–1 teaspoon over each muffin before baking.

SESAME SUGAR
Grind using a pestle and mortar or a coffee grinder 2 Tbsp toasted sesame seeds. Add 2 Tbsp each brown sugar and white sugar, and a pinch salt. Mix or grind briefly. Store in an airtight jar in a cool place. Sprinkle about a teaspoonful over any sweet or bran muffin before baking.

STREUSEL TOPPING
Chop until crumbly, in a food processor or bowl, 1 Tbsp each of cold butter and flour, 2 Tbsp each of sugar and chopped nuts, and $\frac{1}{2}$ tsp of cinnamon. Sprinkle this amount onto 12 medium sweet or bran muffins before baking them.

ORANGE CREAM CHEESE
Mix together until creamy, in a bowl or food processor, $\frac{1}{2}$ cup cream cheese, 2 tsp grated orange, mandarin or tangelo rind and about 3 Tbsp icing sugar. Use in place of butter.

NUTTY CREAM SPREAD
Mix together, as above, $\frac{1}{2}$ cup cream cheese, about 3 Tbsp icing sugar, and $\frac{1}{2}$ cup of very finely chopped, lightly roasted almonds, brazil or cashew nuts, or plain (unroasted) walnuts.

CREAMY HONEY SPREAD
Beat together about $\frac{1}{4}$ cup each butter, creamed honey, and cream cheese. Use as is, or add grated orange rind, spices, or chopped nuts to taste. Refrigerate before use.

MARY ALICE'S RUM BUTTER
Beat or process together 100g softened butter, 1 cup brown sugar, 1 tsp freshly grated nutmeg, and 2 Tbsp rum, until light and creamy. Serve at room temperature. (This is my favourite. I think it wonderful with any sweet or bran muffin.)

BRANDY BUTTER
Replace the rum with brandy in the recipe above, and leave out the nutmeg.

ICING TO DRIZZLE
Sieve $\frac{1}{4}$ cup icing sugar, add, to make a smooth, pourable cream, 1–2 tsp of water, lemon or orange juice, etc. For a "generous drizzle", double these quantities. Pour over hot or warm, not cold, muffins.

Index

Index

Knives by Mail Order

For about 20 years I have imported my favourite, very sharp kitchen knives from Switzerland. They keep their edges well, are easy to sharpen, a pleasure to use, and make excellent gifts. These knives are extremely sharp. Please use them with care until you are used to this.

VEGETABLE KNIFE - $8.00 Pointed, straight edged, 85mm blade, in a plastic sheath. Useful for peeling vegetables and cutting small objects.

UTILITY KNIFE - $9.50 Pointed, 103mm blade which slopes back and comes in a plastic sheath. Used for boning meat and general kitchen use.

SERRATED KNIFE - $9.50 Rounded end, 110mm serrated knife in a plastic sheath. This knife should never require sharpening, it will stay sharp for years and is excellent as a steak knife, for slicing bread and fresh baking, slicing tomatoes and fruit.

THREE PIECE SET - $20.00 Serrated knife (as above), 85mm blade vegetable knife with pointed tip, and (right handed) potato peeler.

GIFT BOX KNIFE SETS - $40.00 Five knives and a (right-handed) potato peeler. Contains straight bladed vegetable knife, blade 85mm; serrated edged vegetable knife, blade 85mm; small utility knife with a pointed tip blade 85mm; small serrated utility 85mm; larger serrated knife with rounded end 110mm (same as above). ("Straight edge" means that the blade is in line with the handle.)

SERRATED CARVING KNIFE - $26.00 Cutting edge 21cm, overall length 33cm. Black, moulded dishwasher- proof handle. Cuts beautifully and never requires sharpening. (Sharpening wears down the serrations.)

STEEL - $20.00 20cm blade, 34cm total length, black, dishwasher-proof handle. Produces excellent results.

For each knife order (of any number of knives) please add $3.50 for packing and postage. All prices inclusive of GST. The prices apply until the end of 1998.

To order send cheque or money order to

Alison Holst Mail Orders
P.O.Box 17-016
Wellington